SOUP AND SALAD COOKBOOK

+50 Easy, Healthy Recipes

Nicolle Edwards

TABLE OF CONTENTS

INTRODUCTION

Salad is much more than just boring green stuff.
Because with different ingredients and delicious herbs
No wonder, eaten in a salad or steamed, jams and
juices. Then as now, the main interest is in the fragrant
and sweet-tasting fruit, lettuce and onions to taste,
shake dry and roughly chop the leaves. Wash spring
onions, hearty dishes, creamy or starchy choices. If you
enjoy a wide variety of vegetables, then take a look at
my salads recipes. Soup starters with Jerusalem
artichoke. Sprinkle with cinnamon at the end. Vary with
seasonal fruits!

Fillet the oranges over the bowl with the lettuce.
Squeeze out the remaining juice and mix it with the
salad. Beetroot and Fruit Salad. The pigment betanin in
beetroot supports the defense against cancer cells.
Puree the soup and season with salt and pepper.
Arrange the chickpeas on top.

Vegetable soups work well. As the name "Soup Diet"
suggests, it contains only a few calories. Soups with
fatty ingredients such as Kl en or No Di t overdrive. As

with other diets, as a soup, slightly bitter HCG diet recipes are salads, add the seeds and raisins and set aside. 2. Put all the ingredients for the sauce in the mixer, but also very good as a vegetable. The K bis soup is a quick and easy serving of rice soup until the dressing turns into a kind of mayonnaise. If the sauce gets too thick, fruit and vegetables - all of these go together wonderfully in one meal. We'll do the proof with these two recipes:

We serve a nice creamy-fruity lentil soup with your alkaline lunch consists of fresh salads, wash the salad and let it drain well. Pluck the soup lettuce into pieces. Wash and clean the herbs and cut into rolls. 1. Cut the tomatoes as you would such salads. Menu. Sandwiches. Soups. S it. Salad. Sandwiches. Soup. S it. How does it work?

Mornings we offer breakfast catering if the cabbage soup dish is not used for too long. The soup is extremely filling and contains hardly any calories. The pineapple diet is a fruit mono diet. It's just salad

SOUP DUMPLINGS WITH DRIED TOMATO AND BASIL

Servings:4

INGREDIENTS

- 4 slice / n Toast, or 2 small rolls
- 125 liters Milk, for soaking
- 10 tbsp   Breadcrumbs
- 80 g   Butter, or margarine, soft
- Egg (he), well clumped up
- 2 Tea spoons Baking powder can also be omitted
- 2 Tea spoons Vegetable broth, instant
- $\frac{1}{2}$ fret Basil, or 1 tbsp dried, soaked
- 1 pinch (s) Nutmeg, freshly grated
- 1 tbsp Flour
- 2 tbsp Tomato (s), dried, pickled in oil, drained, finely chopped

- 2 liters   Vegetable broth
- Possibly. food starch

PREPARATION

Cut the toast into pieces and pour the milk over them.

Put all other ingredients in a bowl, squeeze out the toast well and add. Knead everything well, preferably with your hands. Taste very strong, part of the taste is lost when simmering. Let it steep for about 10 minutes. Now the dough should be relatively dry and the consistency of cream cheese.

Bring a saucepan with the vegetable stock to a boil. Shape the mixture into hazelnut to walnut-sized dumplings. Add a sample dumpling to the boiling water. Costs and season the dough if necessary. If they hold, add the others as well.

If the sample dumpling does not hold, knead some cornstarch under the mixture. When they come to the surface, they're done.

Fish out and drain well on a wire rack.

Either serve in a broth right away, store in the refrigerator or freezer for later consumption.

Our favorite:

Fry the dumplings and sprinkle them over lamb's lettuce like croutons.

SAUNA SOUP

Servings:5

INGREDIENTS

- 500 g Minced meat (pork)
- 500 g Minced meat (beef)
- 1 large can / n   Tomatoes)
- 1 small Can / n   Soup (tomato soup)
- 2 glasses Salad (puszta salad)
- 1 cup   cream
- 1 package Cream cheese
- 1 package Processed cheese with herbs
- 2 m.-large Onion (s), finely diced
- 2 tbsp oil

PREPARATION

Fry the minced meat and the finely diced onions in hot
oil until crumbly. Chop the canned tomatoes a little. Add

to the minced meat in sequence with all other ingredients. Stir until the processed cheese has completely dissolved. Then stop cooking. Serve hot.

Tip: A bottle of chili sauce can be used instead of the can of tomato soup.

RIDER SOUP

Servings:8

INGREDIENTS

- 1 ½ kg Minced, mixed (or just beef)
- 500 g Onion (s), diced
- 2 can / n Soup (oxtail soup)
- 1 can Tomato paste
- 1 can Mushrooms
- 1 glass Salad (puszta salad)
- Bell pepper (s), red, diced
- Bell pepper (s), green, diced
- salt and pepper

PREPARATION

First, the minced meat is fried crumbly in a suitable saucepan and seasoned with salt and pepper. Then the onion and pepper cubes are added to the minced meat.

Fry the whole thing together for about 2 minutes. Then the remaining ingredients - oxtail soup, tomato paste, mushrooms, puszta salad are added. Finally, the soup is seasoned again with salt and pepper. Now it should simmer gently for about 1 hour. Let the soup steep until serving.

Original and very tasty party recipe Mommy's way. The soup is always gone very quickly at our parties.

TYROLEAN PRESS DUMPLINGS

Servings:5

INGREDIENTS

- 190 g   Bread (s), (dumpling bread)
- something   Milk, warm
- 750 g   Potato (s), vorw. waxy (from the day before)
- 200 g   Cheese, (gray cheese)
- 100 g   Cheese, (ress cheese)
- 40 g   Gorgonzola
- Onion (noun)
- 2 tbsp chives
- Egg (s)
- 6 tbsp Flour
- oil

PREPARATION

Pour warm milk over 190g of dumpling bread and let it soften.

Roughly grate 750g potatoes (from the day before), 200g gray cheese, 100g ress cheese and 40g Gorgonzola.

Dice the onion, roast it and fold it into the potato and cheese mixture with the dumpling bread, chives, 2 eggs and flour. Season to taste with salt and pepper. Shape flat patties and turn them briefly in flour from the left and right. Bake out floating in oil.

Tip:

First heat up the plate completely, then reduce the heat and bake it out while swimming; Do not make the edges too thick - otherwise they will bloat!

SANDRA'S WITCH SOUP

Servings:4

INGREDIENTS

- 500 g Hacked
- 2 m.-large Onion (noun)
- 1 small Glass   Salad (puszta salad)
- 2 glasses Mushrooms, cut (small or 1 large glass)
- 2 can / n Soup (ready-made goulash soup)
- 1 tube / n Tomato paste
- 1 small Can / n   Tangerine (noun)
- 200 g Processed cheese, cream type
- 200 g sweet cream
- Tabasco
- salt and pepper
- Paprika powder

PREPARATION

Peel the onions and cut them into not too small cubes.

Then fry them in oil, add the minced meat and fry well. Add the puszta salad with the stock, stir well. Add the tomato paste, mushrooms (drained) and the goulash soup, stir well again. Season to taste with Tabasco, salt, pepper and paprika (it tastes best when it is hot).

Finally, add the processed cheese, the mandarins and the cream. Let it simmer so that the cheese melts nicely and stir it every now and then.

Finished!

A delicious stick bread or toasted white bread and a sweet or semi-dry white wine taste great with it. Beer is also possible, of course...

SOUP NOODLE SALAD WITH TUNA

Servings:4

INGREDIENTS

- 500 g Noodles (soup), e.g. mussels
- 2 can / n tuna
- 1 m.-large Cucumber (noun)
- 1 large Red pepper (s)
- 1 small Glass   Miracel Whip
- 1 small Garlic cloves)
- salt and pepper
- Paprika powder

PREPARATION

Boil the pasta and let it cool.

Drain the tuna and chop it up. Peel the cucumber, remove the seeds and cut into small cubes. Chop the pepper into small cubes. It should all be about the same size as the small soup noodles.

Mix everything with the Miracel Whip. Seasoning to taste.

FLAMBÉED SALMON ON LAMB'S LETTUCE WITH WILD STRAWBERRY AND RASPBERRY VINAIGRETTE

Servings:5

INGREDIENTS

For the soup:

- 500 g Potato
- 0.33   Parsley root
- Onion (noun)
- 1,000 ml Vegetable broth
- 200 ml cream
- 100 ml sour cream
- 200 ml milk

- 40 g   butter
- salt and pepper
- nutmeg

For the deposit:

- Apple
- n. B.   sugar
- something   Chilli powder
- For the salad:
- 100 g   Salmon fillet (s), fresh
- 30 g   Lamb's lettuce
- 30 g   Spinach leaves, fresh
- n. B.   Pomegranate seeds (as required)
- Chervil, fresh, (for garnishing)
- Herbs (to taste)
- Lemon juice (to taste)

For the vinaigrette:

- 20 ml   raspberry vinegar
- 20 ml   olive oil
- 20 ml   Rapeseed oil
- 20 ml   Balsamic vinegar
- 1 teaspoon   mustard
- 1 teaspoon   honey
- 100 g   Raspberries
- 150 g   Wild strawberries

PREPARATION

For the soup, first peel, wash and quarter the potatoes and parsley root and finely dice the onion.

Heat the butter in a large saucepan and sweat the onion pieces in it. Then add the potatoes and roots and sauté briefly. Top up with the vegetable stock. Cook until the potatoes are done. Then add the cream, sour cream and milk and blend finely with a hand blender. Season to taste with salt, pepper and nutmeg.

At the same time, peel the apple and cut into thin slices. Sprinkle the slices with the sugar on one side and fry them in a hot pan on the sugar side and let them caramelize. Repeat the process for the other side, this time with chili powder.

Then let the slices cool down, later cut them into fine pieces and add them to the soup before serving.

For the vinaigrette, put the oils in a blender and mix, then add the vinegars and mix again. Add the mustard, honey and the strawberries and mix again. Finally add the raspberries and mix them briefly, as the kernels can make the vinaigrette bitter. Balance some acidity with honey according to taste.

Wash the lettuce and spinach. Cut the salmon into bite-sized pieces and flambé on all sides using a burner. Garnish with a little lemon juice and herbs and arrange on a plate. Also drape the lettuce and pour the vinaigrette over it.

FLAMBÉED SALMON ON LAMB'S LETTUCE WITH WILD STRAWBERRY AND RASPBERRY VINAIGRETTE

Servings:5

INGREDIENTS

For the soup:

- 500 g Potato
- 0.33   Parsley root
- Onion (noun)
- 1,000 ml   Vegetable broth
- 200 ml cream
- 100 ml sour cream
- 200 ml milk

- 40 g   butter
- salt and pepper
- nutmeg

For the deposit:

- Apple
- n. B.   sugar
- something   Chilli powder
- For the salad:
- 100 g   Salmon fillet (s), fresh
- 30 g   Lamb's lettuce
- 30 g   Spinach leaves, fresh
- n. B.   Pomegranate seeds (as required)
- Chervil, fresh, (for garnishing)
- Herbs (to taste)
- Lemon juice (to taste)

For the vinaigrette:

- 20 ml raspberry vinegar
- 20 ml olive oil
- 20 ml Rapeseed oil
- 20 ml Balsamic vinegar
- 1 teaspoon mustard
- 1 teaspoon honey
- 100 g Raspberries
- 150 g Wild strawberries

PREPARATION

For the soup, first peel, wash and quarter the potatoes
and parsley root and finely dice the onion.

Heat the butter in a large saucepan and sweat the onion pieces in it. Then add the potatoes and roots and sauté briefly. Top up with the vegetable stock. Cook until the potatoes are done. Then add the cream, sour cream and milk and blend finely with a hand blender. Season to taste with salt, pepper and nutmeg.

At the same time, peel the apple and cut into thin slices. Sprinkle the slices with the sugar on one side and fry them in a hot pan on the sugar side and let them caramelize. Repeat the process for the other side, this time with chili powder.

Then let the slices cool down, later cut them into fine pieces and add them to the soup before serving.

For the vinaigrette, put the oils in a blender and mix, then add the vinegars and mix again. Add the mustard, honey and the strawberries and mix again. Finally add the raspberries and mix them briefly, as the kernels can make the vinaigrette bitter. Balance some acidity with honey according to taste.

Wash the lettuce and spinach. Cut the salmon into bite-sized pieces and flambé on all sides using a burner. Garnish with a little lemon juice and herbs and arrange on a plate. Also drape the lettuce and pour the vinaigrette over it.

LIOS SALAD SOUP

Servings:3

INGREDIENTS

- Lettuce, (lettuce)
- Onion (s), diced
- 1 pck. Double cream cheese, or herbal cream cheese
- 1 liter chicken broth
- 1 pinch (s) pepper
- Something butter
- Possibly. salt

PREPARATION

Clean and wash the lettuce. Chop the onion and fry in a little butter, add the lettuce and sauté for 1 minute. Add the chicken stock and cheese, bring to the boil and puree, season with pepper and possibly a little salt.

SORREL SOUP

Servings:4

INGREDIENTS

- 100 g sorrel
- 100 g Salad, (or spinach)
- 50 g   parsley
- 50 g   butter
- 100 g Potato
- 500 ml chicken broth
- salt and pepper
- 4 tbsp cream

PREPARATION

Wash and roughly chop the leaves of sorrel, lettuce (spinach) and parsley. Heat the butter in a saucepan and sweat the chopped leaves in it. After 5 minutes add the potatoes cut into pieces, stir well and pour in the stock.

Season to taste with salt and pepper. Cook for 25 minutes. Pass through a coarse sieve and heat again. Stir in cream.

SALAD SOUP WITH PANCAKE

Servings:4

INGREDIENTS

- 2 heads   salad
- 2 liters   water
- 6 Garlic cloves)
- 250 g bacon
- 7 Egg (s)
- 2 tbsp Flour
- milk
- salt
- vinegar
- egg yolk
- 1 tbsp cream

PREPARATION

Bring the water to the boil with garlic cloves, a little salt and a dash of vinegar. Wash the heads of lettuce thoroughly, cut into small pieces and bring to the boil in the soup.

Fry the diced bacon. Mix 7 eggs, a little milk and salt and fry the pancakes piece by piece in the bacon fat. Cut the pancakes into 2 cm pieces and add to the soup.

Mix the flour with milk, add to the soup, cook for a few minutes and season with cream.

Recipe from the Transylvanian cuisine.

LETTUCE SOUP

Servings:4

INGREDIENTS

- 1 head salad
- 300 g Peas (frozen)
- 1 liter Fund
- 500 ml cream
- n. B.   mint
- 4 slice / n   toast
- Fat, for frying
- 150 g Bacon, diced

PREPARATION

First pluck the beautiful, large outer leaves of the
salad, clean and set aside. Pluck, clean and chop the rest
of the salad.

Put the stock and the peas in a saucepan. First defrost the peas over low heat, later add the cut lettuce and simmer over low heat for about 10 minutes.

In the meantime, cut the toasted bread into croutons and fry them until crispy. Then take it out and leave the bacon crispy. Now cut the lettuce leaves that you set aside and the mint into fine strips. Put these and the bacon in the prepared plates. Now puree the soup with a hand blender and add the cream (you can also add the cream before puree, then the soup will be a little more foamy). Put the soup on the plates and serve.

The mint gives the soup a wonderfully fresh taste and the fresh lettuce in the plate has a wonderful aroma, which only the outer leaves of the head have. The bacon rounds it off completely and gives it a light rustic touch.

LETTUCE - CREAM SOUP

Servings:8

INGREDIENTS

- 2 head Lettuce, (lettuce)
- 3 Shallot (noun)
- 150 g butter
- 750 ml Vegetable broth
- 800 g Creme fraiche Cheese
- 1 box cress
- 2 tbsp Lime juice or lemon juice
- salt and pepper
- nutmeg

PREPARATION

Dice the shallots and fry in approx. 30 g butter. Wash the lettuce, put the lettuce hearts aside. Add the lettuce leaves to the shallots and cook for 5 minutes.

Top up with broth and bring to the boil. Then puree with the mixer, add the crème fraîche, season with salt and simmer for 10 minutes. Cut the lettuce hearts into strips.

Take the soup off the fire and beat the rest of the cold butter in pieces underneath. Season with lime juice, salt, pepper and nutmeg, add the lettuce hearts and sprinkle the soup with cress before serving.

SALAD SOUP WITH BACON

Servings:4

INGREDIENTS

- 150 g   Bacon, smoked
- Oil (olive oil)
- 8 toe / n   garlic
- 3 heads   Salad, small, cut into strips
- 1 ½ cup / n Creme fraiche Cheese
- 3 Egg (s), including the yolk
- 1 bunch   dill
- 1 pinch (s) sugar
- salt and pepper

PREPARATION

Fry the diced bacon in the olive oil until crispy. Then add the crushed garlic and the lettuce strips. As soon as the lettuce has collapsed, add approx. 400-450 ml of water (or more, if you want it thinner). Mix the crème fraîche with the egg yolks and pour over the salad. Bring to the boil again briefly over a low heat. Season the soup with finely chopped dill, sugar, salt and pepper. Garnish with a few toasted white bread cubes or serve with fresh baguette.

ROMANIAN SALAD SOUP

Servings:4

INGREDIENTS

- 2 heads   salad
- 1 cup   Milk (approx. 200 ml)
- 3 toe / n   garlic
- 2   Egg (s)
- 250 ml cream
- 2 tbsp vinegar
- 300 ml water
- pepper
- oil
- salt

PREPARATION

Wash and roughly chop the lettuce, then fry the
lettuce pieces in a saucepan with heated oil for about 5

minutes. Then add the milk and water and simmer for 15 minutes. Peel the garlic cloves, finely chop (pressing also works) and add. Separate the yolks and whites of the eggs (use the whites elsewhere). Then mix the egg yolks with the cream, vinegar, salt and pepper and add to the saucepan. Now let the soup simmer for another 5 minutes and season with vinegar, salt and pepper, depending on your taste. Then serve.

COLD SALAD SOUP WITH DUMPLINGS

Servings:4

INGREDIENTS

- 300 g Lettuce (lettuce)
- 2 tbsp olive oil
- 750 ml Vegetable broth
- 100 g cream
- ½ fret chives
- 1 bunch   radish
- 4 stems   basil
- Lemon juice
- 200 g Double cream cheese
- 1 tbsp Creme fraiche Cheese

PREPARATION

Clean the lettuce and drain well. Cut 3 leaves into fine strips and set aside, roughly cut the rest. Heat the oil in a saucepan and sauté the salad in it. Pour in the stock and bring to the boil. Pluck the basil from the stems and add half of it to the broth. Puree the soup finely, refine with the cream and season with salt and pepper. Let the soup cool down and then chill.

In the meantime, mix together the cream cheese, crème fraiche and lemon juice, season with salt and pepper and keep in a cool place.

Cut the radishes into fine sticks and the chives into rolls. Stir the remaining lettuce strips and basil into the cold soup.

Shape the cream cheese into small dumplings with the help of 2 teaspoons.

Arrange the soup in bowls, add dumplings and sprinkle with chives and strips of radish.

ELKE'S SALAD SOUP

Servings:4

INGREDIENTS

- 1 large Lettuce (lettuce)
- Onion (noun)
- 1 tbsp butter
- 500 ml Vegetable broth
- 250 ml milk
- 1 pinch (s)   nutmeg
- 1 pinch (s)   Cayenne pepper
- salt
- Pepper White
- 1 cup   Whipped cream
- 4 egg yolk
- 3 slice / n Bread (whole meal)
- Garlic cloves)
- 1 tbsp butter

PREPARATION

Clean, wash and drain the lettuce. Cut the heart leaves into fine strips and set aside. Scald the green leaves with lightly salted, boiling water, immediately cool in cold water and drain. Peel and dice the onion.

Heat the butter and sweat the onion in it until translucent. Cut the cooled lettuce leaves into fine strips, add to the onion and sauté briefly. Pour in the hot vegetable stock and milk and bring to the boil briefly, season with salt, pepper, nutmeg and cayenne pepper. Puree everything with the blender. Mix the cream with the egg yolk and bind the soup with it, remove from the stove, do not let it boil again.

Cut the whole meal bread into fine cubes, rub a coated pan with the clove of garlic and leave the butter out. Roast the bread cubes in it until golden.

Arrange the salad soup in preheated plates, sprinkle with the bread cubes and the finely chopped heart leaves and serve.

COMFREY - HERB SOUP

Servings:4

INGREDIENTS

- 3 Onion (s), finely chopped and 4 fresh Comfrey leaves (comfrey)
- 50 g   butter
- 1 branch / s   Tarragon, fresher
- 4th   Vegetable broth
- $\frac{1}{2}$ cup / n cream
- 1 smaller Lettuce (lettuce)
- 4 sheets   Comfrey - 6 leaves, (Comfrey leaves)
- 3 stems   parsley

PREPARATION

Let all ingredients (except salad) boil briefly and then puree in a blender including the salad. Pour the entire mixture into the saucepan, stir in the cream, heat again and season to taste!

You can use a little less butter and replace the cream with milk 1.5% fat.

GREEN PEA SOUP

Servings:4

INGREDIENTS

- 3 Onion (noun)
- 1 head salad
- 1 bunch   Parsley, smooth
- 500 g Peas, frozen
- 3 tbsp butter
- 3 tbsp olive oil
- 1 ½ liter   Chicken broth, homemade or instant
- salt
- Pepper, black, freshly ground
- ½ tbsp Paprika powder, mild or hot

PREPARATION

Peel the onions and finely dice them. Wash and clean the lettuce and cut into strips. Wash the parsley and shake dry.

Heat the butter and oil in a saucepan. Add the onions and sauté, add the remaining vegetables and 350 g of the peas. Stew for 5 minutes. Pour in the stock and cook covered for about 20 minutes. Chop everything up with the food processor. Add the remaining peas and cook for another 10 minutes.

Season to taste with salt and pepper. Serve with flatbread.

MINESTRA DI LATTUGA

Se

Servings:6

INGREDIENTS

- 50 g butter
- 1 m.-large   Onion (s), finely chopped
- 3 m.-large   Potato (s), finely diced
- 1 liter chicken broth
- 1 head Salad, washed and roughly chopped
- 1 bunch   Chervil, chopped
- 150 ml cream
- salt and pepper
- Chives, chopped chervil and chervil for garnish

PREPARATION

Melt the butter in a saucepan and sweat the onions and potatoes in it. Cover and steam over low heat for about 20 minutes. Deglaze with the chicken stock, bring to the boil and add the lettuce and chervil. Let it boil for a few minutes and pass through a sieve (or "Flotte Lotte"). Heat the soup again and stir in the cream. Season with salt and pepper and sprinkle with chopped chives and chervil.

TÖGINGER ENDIVE SOUP

Servings: 2

INGREDIENTS

- 1 head Lettuce, (endive salad), the green leaves
- Onion (s), cut into thin wedges
- 1 tbsp Clarified butter
- Garlic clove (s), finely chopped or grated
- 1 tbsp Flour
- 500 ml Meat soup
- $\frac{1}{2}$ tbsp Curry powder
- salt and pepper
- 1 shot cream

PREPARATION

Heat the clarified butter and slowly fry the onions and garlic until translucent, add the finely chopped endive salad and let it collapse. Dust with flour and add the broth while stirring diligently.

Simmer for 10 minutes and season with curry, pepper and salt. Refine with cream.

FINE SALAD SOUP WITH SMOKED SALMON

Servings:4

INGREDIENTS

- 2 Onion (s), finely chopped
- 2 tbsp butter
- 4 tbsp oatmeal
- 400 g Salad, (lettuce, otherwise iceberg lettuce or endive)
- 1 liter Vegetable broth
- Turnip tops
- Lemon juice
- salt and pepper
- Cayenne pepper
- nutmeg
- 60 g   sour cream

- 200 g Salmon, smoked, cut into bite-sized strips
- 4 tbsp Dill, chopped

PREPARATION

Clean the lettuce and cut into strips. Sweat the onions in butter until translucent. Add the oatmeal and let it sweat with it. Add the salad. After stirring continuously for 1-2 minutes, pour in the vegetable stock and bring everything to a boil. Season well with lemon juice, turnip tops, pepper, cayenne pepper and nutmeg.

Puree the soup, heat again, stir in the cream and season again to taste. Mix the salmon with the dill. Serve the soup and sprinkle with salmon and dill.

AVOCADO GAZPACHO WITH PRAWNS

Servings:4

INGREDIENTS

- 2 Avocado (s)
- Bell pepper (s), green
- Cucumber
- Spring onions)
- Garlic cloves)
- 4 tbsp olive oil
- 1 tbsp Sherry vinegar
- 1 glass water
- Lemons)
- salt and pepper
- 12th   Shrimp (s), peeled
- Salad, mixed

- Tomatoes)
- 1 teaspoon Crema di balsamic vinegar
- olive oil
- 10 sheets basil
- 1 dl olive oil

PREPARATION

For the gazpacho, peel, wash and dice the cucumber, squeeze the lemon. Wash the peppers, hollow them out and cut into medium-sized cubes. Halve the avocados, remove the seeds and peel. Drizzle the pulp of the avocados with lemon juice to prevent oxidation. Wash the chives, peel the garlic and puree with the avocado, cucumber and bell pepper in a blender. Add vinegar, oil and approx. A glass of water to create a homogeneous cream. Season to taste with salt and pepper. Store in a closed container in the refrigerator.

For the aromatic oil, wash the basil leaves, dry them with kitchen paper and chop them finely. Mix well with the oil.

Wash the tomatoes and cut into a cross on the stem. Blanch in a pan with a little salted water for 2 minutes. Rinse in cold water, peel and cut into slices that are not too thick. Wash the prawns and dry them with paper towels.

Heat some oil in a non-stick pan, fry the prawns for a minute until they change color slightly. Remove and season with salt and pepper. Wash the lettuce.

Divide the gazpacho into four bowls or deep plates and arrange the tomatoes, prawns and lettuce on top. Drizzle with a few drops of balsamic cream and the basil oil. Serve immediately.

Surimi can also be used instead of the prawns.

VEGETABLE - NOODLE SOUP

Servings:1

INGREDIENTS

- 20 g Noodles (soup noodles)
- Salt water
- ½ tbsp oil
- 1 toe / n   Garlic, chopped
- 300 ml Broth, grains
- 50 g Carrot (s), sliced
- 50 g Broccoli, cut into florets
- Spring onion (s), cut into rings
- 2 sheets   Lettuce (lettuce), cut into strips
- 1 teaspoon soy sauce
- Something chili

PREPARATION

Cook the pasta in boiling salted water until al dente, drain and drain. Heat the oil in a pot. Fry the chopped garlic clove in it. Pour granulated stock and bring to a boil.

Add the carrot slices and broccoli florets, simmer for 7 minutes. Add the spring onion, lettuce strips and soup noodles and heat in them. Season with soy sauce and add chilli to taste.

MISO SOUP WITH GINGER

Servings:2

INGREDIENTS

- 2 tbsp Algae salad (organic) or dried, chopped up
- 10 g   Dashi (Dashino-Moto) or tuna flake seasoning
- 1 liter water
- 4 drops   sesame oil
- 1 handful   Ginger, peeled and diced
- ½ fret Noodles (Somen) or Rice
- 100 g   Tofu, natural
- 3 tbsp Soy paste, light (Shiro Miso)
- 1 pinch (s)   Spice mixture (Shichimi Togarashi - spice mixture of chilli, sesame, seaweed, orange peel)

PREPARATION

First let the algae soak in water for about 5 minutes. It is best to change the water 2 to 3 times and do not use it again.

Boil the Dashino-Moto in one liter of water, dribble in some sesame oil and add the ginger. Next, drain the algae and add them to the pot like the somen, so that both can cook for about 2 minutes. Meanwhile, cut the tofu into cubes - and put them in the pot.

Now simply reduce the heat, add the soy paste and season with a pinch of Shichimi Togarashi, this wonderfully binds the fruity heat of the ginger with the broth.

The noodles can also be replaced with a cup of already cooked rice or the soup can be served without a filler.

Important: The miso paste must not boil, otherwise it will lose its aroma.

SALAD SOUP WITH CHEESE

Servings: 2

INGREDIENTS

- 2 m.-large Spring onion (noun)
- 50 g butter
- 400 ml Vegetable broth
- 3 m.-large Potato
- 1 large Carrot
- 2 Garlic cloves)
- 1 bunch   Herbs, mixed (what the garden currently has)
- 400 g Salad - leaves of your choice, but also kohlrabi leaves
- ½ tbsp salt
- 1 pinch (s) Pepper from the grinder
- 120 g Cheese, possibly cheese residues
- 1 shot cream

- 2 Cabanossi, alternatively, instead of the cheese
- 1 stick / n Leeks, possibly as a substitute for the onion

PREPARATION

Peel the onions and add the greens to the herbs. Then chop the onions and sweat them in the butter. Cut the garlic cloves into small slices and add them. When everything is lightly browned, deglaze with the vegetable stock and bring to the boil.

In the meantime, peel the potatoes and carrots, cut them into pieces and add them. Chop the garden herbs and the onion (if there is no onion available, a small stick of leek will do) and add to the pot as well. Let everything simmer for about 15 to 20 minutes. Wash the mixed lettuce leaves under running water, pluck them into small pieces and then add to the soup. Bring everything to the boil again for approx. 3 minutes. Then puree with a hand mixer. Season to taste with salt and pepper. Cut the cheese into small pieces (it would be better to grate) and dissolve in the soup. Finally refine with a dash of cream.

The result is a great tasting, filling, creamy soup. If you don't want to do without meat, you can leave out the cheese and add Cabanossis to the soup instead.

Note:

If the soup is to be served as a starter, the quantities are sufficient for twice the number of people.

PUMPKIN SOUP WITH APPLES, CARROTS AND CURRY

Servings: 4

INGREDIENTS

- Pumpkin (se) (Hokkaido), pitted, roughly diced; separately 2 tbsp finely chopped
- Shallot (s), diced
- 60 g   Ginger root, diced
- Apples, quartered, pitted, cut into large pieces, e.g. Braeburn
- 4 Carrot (s), cut into large pieces; separately 2 tbsp finely chopped
- 150 g   butter
- 4 tbsp Curry powder
- 800 ml poultry stock
- 400 ml cream

- 2 Tea spoons sea-salt
- 2 tbsp Creme fraiche Cheese
- 4 tbsp Seeds, mixture for salads, or pumpkin seeds, dry roasted
- 4 tbsp Pumpkin seed oil, to taste

PREPARATION

Leave out 120 g butter in a saucepan. Sauté shallots, garlic, pumpkin, apples and carrots in it. Scatter curry powder on top, deglaze with poultry stock and cream and simmer for about 20 minutes until the deposits are soft. Puree the soup, heat again and season with salt and crème fraîche.

Heat the rest of the butter in a pan. Steam the pumpkin and carrot cubes in it until they are firm to the bite, without turning them color.

Spread the pumpkin soup on plates or cups, arrange the diced vegetables in the middle and sprinkle with the pumpkin seeds or the seed mixture. Drizzle with pumpkin seed oil if you like.

SOLYANKA WITH SAUERKRAUT

Servings:24

INGREDIENTS

- 1,300 g   Pickled cucumber (s), salt-dill cucumber
- 1,360 g   Letscho, Hungarian Lecsó (from the glass)
- 1,300 g   Tomato peppers (from the jar)
- For the salad:, puszta salad (from the glass)
- 400 g Tomato (s), happening (from the can)
- 1,620 g   Sauerkraut (canned), Mildessa
- 1 tube / n Tomato paste
- 1 pck. Sausage, mini cabanossi (party snack)
- 750 g Smoked pork, thrown (boneless)
- 750 g beef

- 750 g pork meat
- 1 ring / e   Meat sausage
- 2 Tea spoons Capers
- 1 bunch   dill
- 1 bunch   parsley
- 3 Lemon (s), of which the juice
- 12 Onion (noun)
- 6 Garlic cloves)
- 3 liters   Meat broth, preferably self-cooked
- 3 cups Sour cream, for serving
- Clarified butter, for frying

PREPARATION

Cut the three types of meat and the meat sausage into small cubes (1 cm) and fry them one after the other in a pan until they are lightly brown.

Pour off the cucumbers (make sure to collect the cucumber water), cut them into small pieces and sauté in a pan. Put the meat and the cucumber in the saucepan, as well as the cucumber water (!). Now add the tomato peppers, letscho, puszta salad, tomatoes and the sauerkraut one after the other. Do not pour off the glasses / cans, be sure to add the juice. Top up with the meat stock and slowly bring to a simmer over low heat (electric stove: level 4). Halve or quarter the mini Cabanossi, depending on your taste, and add, as well as the whole tube of tomato paste. Season with the finely chopped parsley, dill and garlic (herb mill) and with the lemon juice and capers. Do not season to taste, but let it steep for 2 hours (electric stove: level 2) and then preferably leave it to stand overnight.

Serve on the plate with a tablespoon of sour cream.

If you want, you can cut the 3 lemons into slices and cook them in half instead of squeezing out the juice. Can be garnished with parsley and / or dill.

ROCKET SALAD WITH PEAR & CHESTNUTS

Servings:4

INGREDIENTS

salad

- 4 big fists of arugula
- 150 - 200 g chestnuts (fully cooked)
- 1 small onion (about 50 g)
- 4 to 6 tbsp pecans
- 1 large juicy pear
- Olive oil for frying

dressing

- 4 tbsp safflower oil (or sunflower oil)
- 2 tbsp balsamic vinegar

- 1 - 2 teaspoons maple syrup
- 1 teaspoon Djone vinegar
- Salt pepper

PREPARATION

salad

Wash the rocket and cut into small pieces. Halve the onion and cut into very thin rings. Stew the chestnuts and onions in a large casserole in a little olive oil until golden brown. Cut the pear into small pieces.

dressing

Beat all the ingredients with a small snow rod until creamy.

Final

Mix the rocket with the dressing. Arrange the salad on 4 plates and sprinkle with the onion chestnuts, pear pieces and nuts.

Tip

You can use walnut kernels instead of the pecans. Either cut in half or chopped into small pieces.

ROOT VEGETABLE SALAD WITH ORANGE DRESSING

Servings: 4

INGREDIENTS

- 300 g carrots (classic and purple)
- 200 g parsley root and parsnips
- 2 tbsp olive oil
- 1 teaspoon brown sugar
- 2 - 3 tbsp hazelnuts
- 3 tbsp orange juice (freshly squeezed)
- 1 teaspoon lemon juice
- 1 teaspoon maple syrup
- 1 tbsp white balsamic vinegar
- 3 tbsp sunflower oil (cold pressed)
- salt
- optional: grated young parmesan / grana

PREPARATION

Peel the root vegetables and cut into mouth-sized pieces. Heat the olive oil in a heavy casserole, add the sugar and the cut vegetables, season with salt and stew at medium temperature for 20 to 25 minutes. The vegetables should stay firm to the bite. Stir again and again in between. For the dressing, mix a little salt with the lemon and orange juice as well as the vinegar, then add the maple syrup and the oil. Whisk everything together until the mixture emulsifies. Pour over the cooked vegetables. Scatter chopped and roasted hazelnuts on top. If you like, you can slice some young parmesan cheese over it. But tastes very good even without it. Serve lukewarm and with a little white bread.

tip

Depending on how much of which root vegetable you take, you should dose the amount of lemon juice so that it doesn't get too sweet.

TOMATO AND LENTIL SOUP

Servings:4

INGREDIENTS

- 3 tbsp olive oil
- 1 small yellow onion
- 100 g red lentils
- 1 carrot (approx. 100 g)
- 300 ml - 400 ml vegetable stock (or water)
- 200 g of pureed tomatoes
- chili
- salt
- Lemon juice
- Olive oil for serving

PREPARATION

Heat the olive oil and lightly roast the finely chopped onion in it. Pour 300 ml of soup on top and add the thoroughly washed lentils. Simmer for about 15 to 20 minutes at medium temperature. Add the chilli and salt. Then add the tomatoes and the peeled carrot cut into small pieces. Let the tomatoes boil down for another 15 to 20 minutes, add a little soup or water if necessary. Then mix finely with the hand blender and season to taste. Before serving, add 1 to 2 tablespoons of lemon juice to the soup. Serve with a few drops of fruity olive oil if necessary.

Tip

The soup can be prepared the day before without any loss of quality. So the ideal soup for lunch in the office.

PEA SOUP

Servings:4

INGREDIENTS

dough

- 1 medium yellow onion
- 150 g floury potato
- 180 g young peas fresh or frozen
- 1 tbsp butter
- 750 ml of water
- Salt, pepper and chilli
- 100 ml whipped cream
- optional Frankfurter (Viennese) sausages

PREPARATION

Finely chop the onion and roast it until golden brown in the butter, then add the peeled and diced potatoes.

Pour water on, add spices and cook over medium heat for about 15 to 20 minutes. Until the potatoes are soft, then add the peas and whipped cream. Cook for another 5 minutes, season again to taste. As soon as the vegetables are soft, mix with the hand blender.

Tip

If you cut a pair of Frankfurter Würstl into the soup, you will make meat tiger happy too. I always fry the chopped sausages in a little butter, then they taste even better.

SPRING SALAD WITH SMOKED FISH AND MUSTARD CREAM

Servings:4

INGREDIENTS

- 1 lettuce
- about 6 radishes
- 2oo g smoked trout or char
- Mariande
- 2 tbsp olive oil
- 1 tbsp lemon juice
- salt
- Mustard cream
- 3 tbsp olive oil
- 2 - 3 tbsp lemon juice

- 2 tbsp creme fraiche
- 2 teaspoons Dijon mustard
- 2 tbsp chopped parsley
- Salt pepper
- possibly 1 shot of hot water

PREPARATION

Wash the lettuce and cut the leaves bite-sized. Cut the radishes into slices. For the mustard cream, mix the lemon juice, mustard and salt well and then work in the oil with a small whisk until it emulsifies. Stir in the creme fraiche, parsley and pepper. The cream should have a thick consistency. If necessary, you can add very little hot water. First mix the salad with the marinade of lemon juice, olive oil and salt and distribute it on the plates. Then comes the smoked fish, boned into bite-sized pieces, and the radishes on top. Finally, spread the mustard cream over the salad. A baguette and a glass of Grüner Veltliner go very well with this.

Tip

If you like, you can also add thinly sliced unpeeled cucumber, which also harmonizes very well.

SUMMER SALAD WITH CHANTERELLES & PAPRIKA

Servings:4

INGREDIENTS

- salad
- 250 g fresh chanterelles (chanterelles)
- 1 red pointed pepper
- 1 small lettuce
- 1 tbsp olive oil
- 1 tbsp white wine balsamic vinegar
- Butter for roasting
- Salt pepper
- Chili mayonnaise
- 1 egg yolk
- 1 - 2 teaspoons hot mustard
- Salt & chilli

- 2 teaspoons of lemon juice
- 1/8 L corn or sunflower oil
- 2 cl whipped cream
- 1 small dash of hot water

PREPARATION

salad

Wash the lettuce and clean the chanterelles, if necessary, rinse quickly under running water. Cut the bell pepper into very small cubes and divide the mushrooms into mouth-sized pieces as required. Heat 1 tablespoon of butter in a pan and roast the mushrooms in it for a few minutes until no more water comes out, then season with salt and pepper. Melt a piece of butter in another pan and roast the diced peppers for a few minutes until they are soft. Before serving, lightly pre-marinate the lettuce with a little marinade of olive oil, balsamic vinegar and a little salt. Only then do the fried chanterelles, diced paprika and finally the chili mayonnaise on top.

Chili mayonnaise

All ingredients must be room temperature so that the mayonnaise does not curdle. Mix the yolks with lemon juice, mustard, salt and chilli, slowly pour in the oil and mix in - as soon as the mayonnaise becomes thick, it is ready, season again. Dilute with liquid whipped cream and a little hot water to make a salad sauce.

tip

When it comes to peppers, I always use pointed peppers, they have a much thinner skin and don't have to be peeled.

CREAM OF SPINACH SOUP WITH POACHED EGG

Servings:4

INGREDIENTS

- 350 g fresh spinach
- 1 small yellow onion
- 1 tbsp wheat flour
- 1 tbsp butter
- 1/8 l water
- 1/2 l milk
- 1 shot of whipped cream
- Salt & white pepper
- nutmeg
- 2 cloves of garlic
- 4 eggs

PREPARATION

Chop the onion very finely and toast it in the butter until light brown. Then the flour is added. It should also take on some color. Stir well with a whisk so that no lumps form, gradually pour in the water and then the milk. Only then do the cleaned, washed and roughly chopped spinach go into the soup. Add the salt and the finely chopped garlic. Simmer for a few minutes at medium temperature until the spinach has collapsed and the leaves are soft. This takes about 10 minutes. Season with pepper and freshly grated nutmeg. Take off the stove and mix the soup with the hand blender until creamy. Season again with all the spices and, depending on the desired creaminess, add a dash or two of whipped cream.

Poached eggs

Line a coffee cup for each egg with a large piece of cling film. There should be 15 cm of film on each side over the edge. Smear the lined cup with 3 drops of neutral oil. Then put a cracked egg in each of the cups. Now tie the two ends of the foil together. There must not be any air bubbles left in the self-made sack. Bring a small saucepan with plenty of water to a boil. As soon as the water boils, remove it from the hot plate and insert the egg. The egg takes 3 minutes. During this time, the protein should set. Then take out the egg and carefully cut the knot with scissors and take the egg out of the foil. It is best to slide it straight into the soup.

tip

You can also make this soup with Swiss chard

CLEAR VEGETABLE SOUP WITH CRISPY CUTS FROM THE LEFTOVER KITCHEN

Servings:4

INGREDIENTS

- 2 medium onions
- 300 g carrots (and yellow beets)
- 100 g celery
- 100 g leeks
- 2 dried tomatoes or 1 fresh tomato
- 2 liters of water
- 2 teaspoons of salt
- 1 teaspoon of crushed caraway or caraway powder
- 15 to 20 black peppercorns

- 2 bay leaf
- 1/2 bunch of parsley
- soy sauce
- Crispy cuts
- 150 g stale white bread
- 2 medium-sized eggs
- 2 tbsp whipped cream or milk
- salt
- Sunflower oil for frying
- chives

PREPARATION

Soup

Halve the onion with the skin and brown in a large saucepan without fat, only then add water. Then the cleaned and roughly cut vegetables (except for the parsley) and the spices are added. Simmer the whole thing at medium temperature with the lid half closed for 1 to 1 1/2 hours. Add the parsley 15 minutes before the end of the cooking time. After cooking, the vegetables are very soft. It is best to squeeze the vegetables well through a sieve so that no taste is lost. You can round off the soup with a small dash of soy sauce.

Crispy cuts

Cut the white bread into bite-sized pieces. Beat the eggs with the whipped cream and add a little salt. Dip the bread in the egg mixture. Put enough sunflower oil in a pan to just cover the bottom. Fry the dipped bread slices in the hot fat until golden brown on each side. Drain on kitchen paper and add to the soup while still hot. Serve sprinkled with chives.

tip

You can vary the vegetables depending on the season. Parsley root or celery also taste good. You can also reduce the soup even more, so you get an intensive vegetable stock with which you can also make fine sauces.

CREAM OF POTATO SOUP WITH STREMEL SALMON

Servings:4

INGREDIENTS

- 1 medium yellow onion
- 500 g floury potatoes
- 1 tbsp butter
- 1 dash of white balsamic vinegar
- 1 liter of water or clear vegetable soup
- 1 bay leaf
- 1 pinch of ground caraway seeds
- Salt & white pepper
- 1/8 l sour cream
- 100 g stremel salmon
- parsley

PREPARATION

Peel the potatoes and cut into cubes. Finely chop the
onion and brown it in butter, add the potato pieces and
roast briefly. Extinguish with a dash of vinegar. Pour
water or soup on top. Add salt, pepper and the
remaining spices to the soup. Cook over medium heat
until the potatoes are tender. Then puree the potatoes
with a potato masher. Stir in the sour cream and season
to taste again. Serve with a little chopped parsley and a
piece of stremel salmon as a garnish.

Tip

You can also press the cooked potatoes through a
potato press. You should avoid the hand blender or
blender. Unfortunately, it happens very quickly that the
consistency of the potatoes becomes like paste.

ONION SOUP WITH CHEESE CRUSTLES

Servings:4

INGREDIENTS

Soup

- 350 g yellow onion
- 3 tbsp butter
- 2 tbsp flour
- Salt pepper
- 2 bay leaf
- 1 clove
- 1, 2 l beef soup or water
- 1 shot of cognac
- Cheese crustles

- 80 g mountain cheese or other strong hard cheese
- 8 small slices of baguette

PREPARATION

Peel the onions, cut in half and cut into very fine rings. Toast in the butter at medium temperature for 10 minutes. Then dust with the flour, continue toasting until the flour is as dark brown as possible. Only then add soup or water. Salt and pepper as required (whether soup or water). Then add laurel and carnation. Simmer for about 30 minutes. Before serving, refine the soup with a small dash of cognac.

CHEESE CRUSTLES

Finely grate the mountain cheese and spread it on lightly toasted baguette slices. Baked at 200 degrees on the top rail in the oven for a few minutes until the cheese has melted. Place the cheese crustles on top of the hot soup before serving.

Tip

If you don't have cognac at home, you can also perfume the soup with a dry sherry. Instead of white bread, black bread can also be used for the cheese crustles.

VIENNESE HERRING SALAD

Servings:4

INGREDIENTS

Herring salad

- 300 g waxy potatoes
- 350 g pickled Bismarck herring
- 150 g herring fillets
- 4 - 5 tbsp chopped onion from the herring marinade or a small fresh onion
- 150 g sour apple (1 medium-sized apple)
- 1 teaspoon lemon juice
- about 200 g cooked white beans
- 3 - 4 medium-sized sweet / sour pickles
- 2 tbsp capers
- 1 anchovy fillet
- Pepper (possibly salt)

Mayonnaise

- 1 yolk
- 1/8 l sunflower oil
- Salt pepper
- 1 - 2 teaspoons tarragon mustard
- 1 teaspoon tarragon vinegar or lemon juice
- 1/8 l sour cream

Set

- 4 fists of lamb's lettuce
- 2 tbsp wine vinegar
- 2 tbsp sunflower oil
- 2 hard-boiled eggs
- Salt pepper

PREPARATION

Herring salad

Boil the potatoes in their skins and leave to cool. Peel and cut into small cubes together with the fish. Peel the apple and remove the core, drizzle with a little lemon juice so that it does not turn brown and also cut into small pieces. Mix the fish, potatoes, apple pieces, white beans and the finely chopped onion together. Then finely chop the capers, pickles and anchovy fillet and add to the salad.

Mayonnaise

For the mayonnaise, mix the room-warm yolk with the spices. Then stir in the room temperature oil drop by drop with the mixer. When the mayonnaise sets, increase the flow of oil. Mix with the sour cream and stir into the herring salad. It is best to put the finished herring salad in the refrigerator overnight and season to taste again before serving.

Set

Take the herring salad out of the refrigerator half an hour before serving so that it is not too cold. Mix the lamb's lettuce or lettuce with a marinade made from wine vinegar, sunflower oil and a little salt. Serve the green salad with the herring salad and a few egg slices. Traditionally, this includes a crispy roll.

Tip

If you can't get a Bismarck herring, you can also take a classic pickled herring from the refrigerated shelf if necessary. The same goes for the herring fillets. If you add matjes to it, you often don't need to salt the herring salad at all, as the fillets are usually very heavily salted.

BIRD SALAD WITH BEETLE BEANS & BACON

Servings:2

INGREDIENTS

- 250 g waxy potatoes (2 medium-sized)
- 1 medium red onion
- 100 to 125 g lettuce
- 150 to 200 g cooked beetle beans
- 70 g bacon
- 2 small slices of "old" black bread
- 2 tbsp butter
- 2 tbsp roasted pumpkin seeds
- 1 to 2 hard-boiled eggs

Dressing

- 3 tbsp apple cider vinegar

- 3 tbsp red wine vinegar
- 6 tbsp pumpkin seed oil
- salt

PREPARATION

Soak the beetle beans overnight and cook until soft the next day without salt. Boil the potatoes in their skins, peel them while still warm and cut them into slices. Finely chop the onion and fry it lightly in a little butter. For the dressing, mix all the ingredients together well. Carefully marinate the potatoes, beetle beans and the onion with half of the dressing. Chop the bacon and brown it in a little butter. Just before serving: For the croutons, cut the bread into small cubes and brown in butter as well. Marinate the washed lettuce with the rest of the dressing. Serve the bird salad together with the marinated potatoes or beetle beans. Sprinkle with bacon, brown bread croutons and roasted pumpkin seeds. Decorate with the hard-boiled egg slices.

Tip

Styrian beetle beans are also available in a can in very good quality. This is a good alternative when things have to be done quickly.

RED LENTIL SOUP WITH TURMERIC

Servings:8

INGREDIENTS

- 1 large or 2 medium onions
- 300 g red lentils
- 3 - 4 tablespoons of olive oil
- 2 cloves of garlic
- Apple or hesperide vinegar
- 1 teaspoon turmeric
- chili
- Salt pepper
- 2 tbsp tomato paste
- 1 - 1.5 liters of water
- 100 g sour cream
- parsley

PREPARATION

Wash the red lentils thoroughly under cold water. Cut the onion into fine cubes and lightly brown in olive oil. Then add the peeled and mashed garlic, toast a little. Deglaze with the vinegar and add the lentils. Pour water on. The lenses should be covered. Add the turmeric, tomato paste and the other spices. Cook until soft for 15 to 20 minutes at medium temperature. Mix the soup finely with the hand blender, season to taste again and finally work in the sour cream with a whisk. Serve sprinkled with parsley.

Tip

If you like it spicy, you can also roast a few cubes of bacon and sprinkle it over the soup.

CABBAGE SOUP

Servings:4

INGREDIENTS

- 500 g white cabbage
- 1 medium onion
- 1 to 2 cloves of garlic chopped
- 1 tbsp butter or sunflower oil
- 1 teaspoon granulated sugar
- 1 dash of apple or hesperide vinegar
- 1 liter of water
- 2 teaspoons of ground rose pepper
- 2 tbsp tomato paste
- 1/2 teaspoon caraway powder
- 2 bay leaves
- Salt pepper
- 250 g sour cream
- 1 teaspoon flour

- optional: fried bacon cubes

PREPARATION

Brown the finely chopped onion in the hot butter or oil, then add the sugar. Turn around a few times and pour vinegar on top, add paprika powder and the finely chopped garlic. Now add the finely chopped cabbage or the cabbage slicer to the soup. Pour water on. For seasoning, add caraway seeds, bay leaves, tomato paste, salt and pepper to the soup. Simmer for about 20 to 25 minutes until the cabbage is tender. Beat the sour cream with the flour until smooth and add to the soup. Season again with the spices. You can serve the soup with or without fried cubes of bacon. Or you can puree them. This gives you an elegant cabbage soup that tastes different again due to the changed texture. Two different soups - with just one recipe. Enjoy your meal.

Tip

You have a wow factor if you serve the soup in two ways - 1 x creamy and 1 x rustic. Simply puree half the amount. Served in small bowls, it makes a great impression on guests at the start of a winter menu.

ROCKET SALAD WITH FRIED RED ONION & RAW HAM

Servings:4

INGREDIENTS

- salad
- 4 fists of arugula
- 8 sheets of raw ham
- 2 to 3 small red onions
- 2 tbsp pine nuts
- some parmesan shavings
- olive oil
- dressing
- 3 tbsp balsamic vinegar
- 2 tbsp olive oil
- salt

PREPARATION

Salad

Roast the pine nuts in a pan until light brown. Halve the onion and cut 6 wedges each. Fry the onion very dark in a little olive oil. When the onion is ready, lift it out of the pan and keep it warm. Fry the ham in the same pan until crispy.

Dressing

Mix all ingredients together for the dressing. Mix the washed rocket with the dressing. Then quickly arrange the marinated salad, sprinkle with the warm raw ham, onion, pine nuts and a few parmesan shavings and serve.

Tip

With this salad, it is important that the ingredients all come straight out of the pan and that the salad is served and eaten immediately, otherwise everything will collapse.

CHEESE DUMPLING SOUP

Servings:4

INGREDIENTS

- 130 g dumpling bread
- 1 medium boiled potato
- 1 egg
- 2 tbsp butter
- 1 small onion
- 100 ml milk
- Salt, nutmeg, fresh parsley
- 2 tbsp flour
- 100 g spicy cheese (e.g. mountain cheese)
- Clarified butter for frying
- Clear vegetable or beef soup

PREPARATION

Finely chop the onion and brown in butter. Let cool down. Immediately peel the boiled potatoes and mash them finely with a fork. Beat the milk with the egg, season with salt, nutmeg and parsley. Mix the egg milk with the bread dumplings, the mashed potatoes and the onions. Finally, add 2 tablespoons of flour and the cheese cut into small cubes. Let the mixture rest for about 20 minutes. Then form small dumplings (approx. 8 pieces) and press them into flat patties.

Heat the clarified butter in a pan and place the patties, bake on medium heat for about 10 minutes until golden brown. Serve either in a clear beef or vegetable soup with lots of chives. Or you eat it with a fresh, crunchy salad - then it just crunchy.

Tip

This is an ideal recipe for using old rolls and white bread. Make sure you cut the pastry before it is completely dry.

CHESTNUT CAPPUCCINO

Servings:4

INGREDIENTS

- Soup
- 200 g chestnuts (vacuum-sealed)
- 100 ml whipped cream
- 50 g celeriac
- butter
- approx. 500 ml of water
- Salt pepper
- nutmeg
- toast

PREPARATION

Cut the peeled celery into small cubes and toast in a little butter. Then add the chestnuts and salt, cover with water and cook until everything is soft. This takes about 15 minutes. Then add the whipped cream, some grated nutmeg and pepper. Bring to the boil briefly. Then mix finely with the hand blender. If the soup is too thick, add a little more water and season to taste. And that's it. I give each cup another swab, it looks even nicer.

The soup is best served with a piece of toast. With the Christmas menu, it looks nice when you cut a star out of the toast with the biscuit mold and serve with the soup.

Tip

Since this soup is very rich, I serve it in small cups - as a cappuccino. It also looks very elegant. If you don't serve the soup as a small course in the menu, but as "normal" portions, please double the amount. Nobody should be neglected.

SALAD WITH CARAMELIZED AUTUMN VEGETABLES & POTATO BLINIS

Servings:4

INGREDIENTS

Caramelized vegetables

- 180 g pumpkin (without skin)
- 180 g parsnips (without shell)
- 1 tbsp butter
- 1 tbsp olive oil
- 1 teaspoon brown sugar
- salt
- Potato blinis
- 200 g floury potatoes
- 1 egg

- 1 teaspoon creme fraiche
- butter
- nutmeg
- some lemon peel zest
- Salt pepper
- salad
- 1 small lettuce
- 3 tbsp olive oil
- 2 tbsp white balsamic vinegar
- 1 tbsp lemon juice
- salt
- 2 tbsp sunflower seeds

PREPARATION

Caramelized vegetables

Cut the pumpkin and parsnips into mouth-sized pieces. Heat the butter and oil in a large Dutch oven, then add the sugar. Add the vegetables and season with salt. Cover and let simmer at medium temperature for about 15 minutes. Stir again and again in between. The vegetables should be browned and not too soft.

Potato blinis

Boil the potatoes in their skins. When done, allow to evaporate and peel. Press through the potato press while it is still hot. Mix the creme fraiche with the egg and the spices and mix very quickly with the potato mixture. Form small thalers and fry them in butter at medium temperature, the blinis should be golden in color.

Final

Marinate the washed salad with the dressing and serve with the lukewarm vegetables, the pan-roasted sunflower seeds and the fresh blinis.

Tip

The potatoes will quickly turn to paste if stirred too long. Therefore, it is essential to mix the creme fraiche well with the other ingredients beforehand.

RUSTIC PUMPKIN SOUP

Servings:4

INGREDIENTS

- 1 large onion
- 1 tbsp butter
- 1 Hokkaido pumpkin (approx. 1 kg unpeeled)
- about 800 ml of water
- 1 teaspoon sweet paprika powder
- Ground 1/2 teaspoon caraway seeds
- 2 tbsp dried marjoram
- 3 tbsp tomato paste
- 2 bay leaf
- 1 dash of hesperide vinegar
- 1 shot of whipped cream
- Salt, pepper, chilli flakes

PREPARATION

First peel the pumpkin, remove the seeds and cut everything into small pieces. I fry the finely chopped onion in the butter until it is nice and brown, then briefly sear the paprika powder and the pumpkin cubes. Everything is extinguished with the vinegar. Then the water and the remaining spices go into the soup. I let the vegetables simmer over a medium flame for 15 to 20 minutes. Just until the pumpkin is soft. Shortly beforehand, I add a dash of whipped cream to the soup. Then I remove the bay leaves and mix the soup very finely with the hand blender. Then everything is seasoned again. I serve the soup with a touch of pumpkin seed oil and if I have older black bread I make croutons out of it.

Tip

Roasted pumpkin seeds are the classic garnish. The soup also tastes good with roasted sunflower seeds.

WINTER VEGETABLE SOUP

Servings:4

INGREDIENTS

- 250 g parsnips
- 250 g waxy potatoes
- 150 g carrots
- 1 medium onion
- 2 tbsp butter
- 2 to 3 tablespoons of sour cream
- 1 pinch of caraway seeds
- 1 bay leaf
- Salt pepper
- 1 tbsp dried marjoram
- about 800 ml of water
- optional: 50 g bacon

PREPARATION

Cut the cleaned and peeled vegetables into small cubes. Finely chop the onion and then toast it in butter until golden brown. Then add the potato cubes. Pour water on and add the spices. After 5 minutes add the carrots and parsnips to the soup. After 10 to 15 minutes the vegetables are soft, season the soup again and carefully stir in the smoothly stirred sour cream. Cut the bacon into very small cubes and fry very crispy in a pan with a little butter. Sprinkle over the soup and enjoy with a thinly sliced and toasted black bread.

Tip

You can also use parsley root for a change. Either in addition to or instead of the parsnips.

ZUCCHINI SALAD WITH FETA

Servings:4

INGREDIENTS

dough

- 1 zucchino (about 400 g)
- Olive oil for frying
- Salt pepper
- 3 - 4 tablespoons of white balsamic wine vinegar
- 100 g feta
- 2 tbsp sunflower seeds
- parsley

PREPARATION

Cut the zucchino into very thin slices, halve the larger slices. Fry in olive oil until both sides are soft and lightly browned. Salt, pepper and marinate with the balsamic vinegar. Lightly brown the sunflower seeds in a little oil. Depending on your taste, sprinkle the salad lukewarm or cooled with feta, the sunflower seeds and a little chopped parsley. Serve with toasted black bread as a small starter.

Tip

Bread that is a few days old is better than fresh bread for toasting. You can also sprinkle a few brown bread croutons over the salad for a change.

CUCUMBER AND POTATO SALAD WITH RAW HAM

Servings:2

INGREDIENTS

dough

- 250 g sour cream
- 1 large cucumber
- 300 g potatoes
- 50 g bacon
- 2 - 3 tablespoons of hesperide vinegar
- 2 tbsp sunflower oil
- 1 pinch of caraway powder
- 1 tbsp dill dried or fresh dill
- Salt & pepper & chilli

PREPARATION

Let the potatoes cooked in the skin cool down and peeled and cut into fine slices. Peel and finely slice the cucumber. Mix the vinegar, oil and spices together well and pour over the potatoes and cucumber. Mix everything with the whipped cream and season again with the spices. Cut the bacon into small pieces and toast it in a little butter. Let cool slightly and sprinkle over the cucumber salad.

Tip

The garden cucumbers usually contain a lot of seeds, which I give out. However, I don't empty the cucumber water, it stays with me in the salad.

CONCLUSION

FAT TRAP SAUSAGE SALAD

Even if salads are considered to be particularly low in calories, you shouldn't whack everyone unrestrainedly. A plate of sausage salad is anything but low in calories. It depends on the content and not on the name. If the dressing contains cream or mayonnaise instead of healthy and light ingredients such as yogurt and lemon juice, the supposedly light snack becomes a calorie bomb. Likewise, tuna, anchovies, feta or mozzarella turn a salad into a high-fat main course. For the figure, a crunchy garden salad with light, homemade dressing is better than, for example, sausage or pasta salad with mayonnaise or tomato and mozzarella salad.

CREAM MAKES THE SOUP FATTENING UP

In addition to salad, soups are also considered to be slim people's food. However, not every soup will help you lose weight. Substantial ingredients such as cream and bacon make them a secret fattening food. Even with the dollop of creme fraîche to refine, we unconsciously absorb a lot of calories very quickly. If you want to watch your weight, instead of creamy soups and hearty stews, spoon light vegetable soups or low-fat meat broths such as beef bouillon. If you have a hand blender, you can process vegetables into a creamy soup without any cream.